GLOBE FEARON

LITERATURE

LANGUAGE ENRICHMENT WORKBOOK

▪ *Silver Level* ▪

Upper Saddle River, New Jersey
www.globefearon.com

Supervising Editor: Karen McCollum
Editor: Amy Greenberg
Editorial Developer: Pearson Education Development Group
Production Editor: Travis Bailey
Associate Production Editor: Amy Benefiel
Designer: Angel Weyant
Manufacturing Supervisor: Mark Cirillo

ISBN 0-130-23577-6

Printed in the United States of America

1 2 3 4 5 6 7 8 9 10 04 03 02 01 00

CONTENTS

TO MY DEAR AND LOVING HUSBAND

A. **Write words that rhyme with the words listed.**

fan   see   mold   today

_______   _______   _______   _______
_______   _______   _______   _______
_______   _______   _______   _______

B. **Complete the lines of the poem using the following words.**

we	pray	hold	recompense
man	persever	can	ever
quench	repay	thee	gold

To My Dear and Loving Husband

by Anne Bradstreet

If ever two were one, then surely _______________;

If ever man were loved by wife, then _______________;

If ever wife was happy in a _______________,

Compare with me, ye women, if you _______________,

I prize thy love more than whole mines of _______________,

Or all the riches that the East doth _______________.

My love is such that rivers cannot _______________,

Nor ought but love from thee give _______________.

Thy love is such I can no way _______________,

The heavens reward thee manifold, I _______________.

Then while we live in love let's so _______________

That when we live no more we may live _______________.

SONG CONCERNING A DREAM OF THE THUNDERBIRDS

bright	multi-colored	golden	sharp
huge	black	billowing	glowing
red	rising	fierce	wild
quick	enormous	stretching	soaring

A. Write adjectives to describe these parts of a thunderbird. Choose from the list above or find your own adjectives.

1. Eyes _______________________   _______________________

2. Wings _______________________   _______________________

3. Claws _______________________   _______________________

4. Head _______________________   _______________________

5. Feathers _______________________   _______________________

B. How would you describe the land of the thunderbirds? Write adjectives that describe these parts of the land. Choose from the list above or find your own adjectives.

1. Clouds _______________________   _______________________

2. Sky _______________________   _______________________

3. Wind _______________________   _______________________

4. Land _______________________   _______________________

5. Hills _______________________   _______________________

C. Write your own poem, using some of the descriptive words you have written above.

____

____

____

____

____

SPEECH IN THE VIRGINIA CONVENTION

A. Reread Patrick Henry's speech in your textbook. Circle the number of the sentence below that tells what is said in each paragraph.

Paragraph One:
1. Patrick Henry feels that it is important to speak his opinion truthfully.
2. Patrick Henry feels that it is important to hold back his angry feelings right now.

Paragraph Two:
1. It is best to hope that everything will be all right in the future.
2. It is best to plan for the terrible future that might come.

Paragraph Three:
1. The British will use their fleets and armies to control us.
2. My experience tells me that we can trust the British because they are our friends.

Paragraph Four:
1. We are the only enemy Great Britain has in this part of the world.
2. Great Britain's armies and navies will protect us.

Paragraph Five:
1. We must plead and beg with the British.
2. There is no use trying to talk to the British anymore.

Paragraph Six:
1. Maybe the King will listen to us.
2. We have begged and protested.

Paragraph Seven:
1. The best way to be free is to wish to be free.
2. We must fight to keep our rights.

Paragraph Eight:
1. We will not be weak next week or next year.
2. If we wait, it will be too late to fight.

Paragraph Nine:
1. We will not be weak if we have many people, if God is with us, if we are brave, and if we have no choice.
2. We are not weak because we have many people, because God is with us, because we are brave, and because we have no choice.

Paragraph Ten:
1. The war has already begun because the British are here with their armies and navies.
2. The war has already started because we stand idle.

B. On a separate sheet of paper, write the ten correct sentences in one paragraph.

FAREWELL ADDRESS

A. Fill in the missing words from Washington's "Farewell Address."

Introduction:

> affairs   second   candidate   advice

1. My _______________ term as President will soon be over.

2. I will not be a _______________ for reelection.

3. The foreign and domestic _______________ of our country are in order.

4. Therefore, I will offer you some _______________ .

Body:

> unity   party   regional
>
> courts   tyrant   power

5. It is the _______________ of government which is the source of your real independence.

6. _______________ loyalties are a danger to your liberty.

7. You have seen how _______________ rivalry in France led to chaos there.

8. The public, when everything turns to chaos, might give full _______________ to one strong leader.

9. Sooner or later, this leader will become a _______________ .

10. Fortunately, we have three branches of power, the President, the Congress, and the _______________ .

Conclusion:

> against   avoid   European

11. Therefore, _______________ party allegiance, guard _______________ selfish interest, and avoid entanglement in _______________ affairs.

B. On a separate sheet of paper, rewrite the completed sentences in three paragraphs: introduction, body, and conclusion.

LETTER TO HER DAUGHTER FROM THE NEW WHITE HOUSE

A. In her letter to her daughter, Abigail Adams writes about her trip to Washington, DC, and her first impressions of the new city. Fill in the missing words of these sentences.

human being	glass	buildings	bells
woods	wood	clothes	name

1. A person can get lost in the ________________ on the way to Washington.

2. It is a city only in ________________ .

3. The small houses you see on the way don't have ________________ windows.

4. On the road to Washington, you can travel for miles without seeing any other ________________ .

5. In Washington, the ________________ are not all finished and they are scattered.

6. She wishes there were some ________________ hanging in the house so she can call the servants.

7. There is not enough ________________ to keep the fires going.

8. She has no place to hang the ________________ to dry.

B. Abigail Adams names a few positive impressions that the new city and her new home make on her. Fill in the missing words.

fires	crimson	thirty	vessels	spot

1. Many ________________ go up and down the river.

2. The house is so large, it requires ________________ servants.

3. There are many ________________ in the house to warm us and to cheer us.

4. The room with the ________________ furniture in it is a very handsome room.

5. The house is in a beautiful ________________ .

C. On a separate piece of paper, write a letter to a friend or relative describing your first impressions of a place you visited for the first time.

from THE AUTOBIOGRAPHY/
from POOR RICHARD'S ALMANACK

A. Number the following events from Franklin's *The Autobiography* **in chronological order.**

________ I could not find any work in Boston.

________ In 1720 or 1721, my brother began to print a newspaper in Boston.

________ When I was still a boy, I wrote articles for my brother's newspaper.

________ I left my brother's newspaper business and began looking for a new job in Boston.

________ Three days later, I landed in New York.

________ At Amboy, I had a fever.

________ In New York, Mr. Bradford suggested that I go to Philadelphia.

________ I left secretly by boat for New York without saying goodbye.

________ From New York, I took a boat to Amboy.

________ From Amboy, I walked fifty miles to Burlington, New Jersey.

B. Fill in the missing word to complete each aphorism from *Poor Richard's Almanack.*

makes	sink	instruct	dares	stink
sleeping	country	early	slow	fine

1. The things which hurt, _______________ .

2. Beware of little expenses; a small leak will _______________ a great ship.

3. Fish and visitors _______________ after three days.

4. The worst wheel of the cart _______________ the most noise.

5. At the working man's house, Hunger looks in, but _______________ not enter.

6. _______________ to bed and _______________ to rise, makes a man healthy, wealthy, and wise.

7. Be _______________ in choosing a friend, slower in changing.

8. Sally laughs at everything you say. Why? Because she has _______________ teeth.

9. A _______________ man between two lawyers is like a fish between two cats.

10. The _______________ fox catches no poultry.

WHAT IS AN AMERICAN?

A.   These sentences are taken from the essay by Jean de Crèvecoeur. What new ideas can you add to the essay? Write your own ideas in each of the blank spaces.

What is an American, this new man? He is a person from

_________________ or the descendant of a person from _______________.

In America, individuals of all nations intermarry and form a new nationality. Their ______________ and ______________ will one day cause great changes in the world. Americans are pilgrims. They are carrying with them the ______________ and ______________ of all of their ancestors.

In America, ______________ will be quickly rewarded. No cruel ______________, rich ______________, or mighty ______________ will demand to share their riches.

The American is a new man. He must, therefore, listen to new ______________ with an open ______________ and form new ______________. This is an American.

B.   Where did you or your ancestors come from? Are you changing or did your ancestors change any of their ways of doing things when they came to the United States? Explain your answer.

____

____

____

____

____

____

____

____

____

SUNRISE IN HIS POCKET/ GODASIYO, THE WOMAN CHIEF

A. Fill in the blanks with the words from the list to re-create Davy Crockett's very, very tall tale.

sun	grunt	oyster	shake
bear	ice	walked	sparks
pour	face	fire	thunderclouds

Here is what I did on the day the _____________ froze. One January morning, it was so cold the trees were too stiff to _____________. Well, I decided the only way I was going to get some _____________ was to make it myself. I brought my knuckles together like two _____________, but the _____________ froze before I could collect them.

The sun had gotten jammed between cakes of _____________ under the wheels of the earth. It was so cold that my teeth and tongue were all collapsed together as tight as an _____________. I beat a bear against the ice until the hot oil began to _____________ out of it on all sides. I squeezed the hot _____________ oil until I'd thawed the earth loose. Then I poured about a ton of the hot bear oil over the sun's _____________.

In about fifteen seconds, the earth gave a _____________ and began to move. The sun _____________ up into the sky. It saluted me and I saluted back.

B. Listed below are some of the interesting objects that are named in the story "Godasiyo, the Woman Chief." Read the story and then decide to which group each of the objects belongs.

tree limbs   venison   dried fruits   dried berries   saplings

NATIVE-AMERICAN FOOD	MATERIALS USED TO BUILD THE BRIDGE
_________________________	_________________________
_________________________	_________________________
_________________________	_________________________

from MY BONDAGE AND MY FREEDOM

Writers know the difference between a negative and positive connotation of a word. For example, Frederick Douglass, in *My Bondage and My Freedom,* says that Mrs. Auld was an *intelligent* woman. This word has a positive connotation. If he had used either of the following words, Douglass would have created a negative connotation: *cunning, shrewd.*

A.   Look at the words below. Draw a line matching words of similar meaning. Then circle all the words that have a more positive connotation. Use a dictionary if you need to. The first one is done for you as an example.

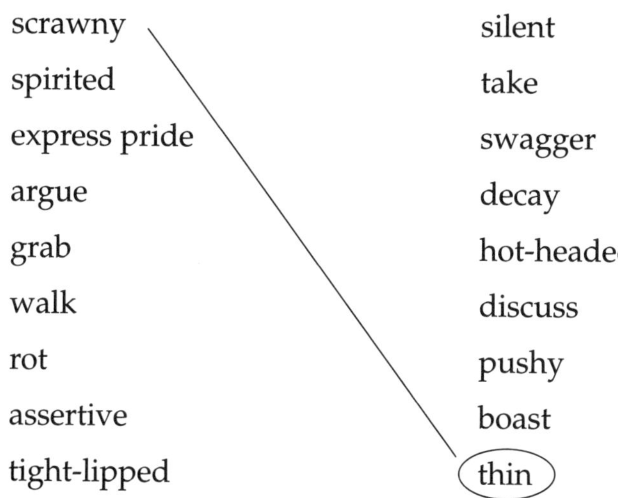

B.   Choose four pairs of the words above. Use them in sentences to show their differences.

Here's an example:
    The girl is thin, so she was a good runner.
    That person is so scrawny that she probably hasn't eaten a good meal for weeks.

1. ____

____

2. ____

____

3. ____

____

4. ____

____

SILVER LEVEL, Unit 2 ■ 9

AIN'T I A WOMAN?

A. Synonyms are words with similar meanings. Give at least two synonyms for each of the following words which are taken from "Ain't I a Woman?" Use a dictionary or thesaurus, if necessary. The first one is completed as an example.

1. look   _____watch_____   _____see_____   _____observe_____

2. children   _____________   _____________   _____________

3. talking   _____________   _____________   _____________

4. work   _____________   _____________   _____________

5. cried   _____________   _____________   _____________

6. strong   _____________   _____________   _____________

7. asking   _____________   _____________   _____________

8. let   _____________   _____________   _____________

9. helped   _____________   _____________   _____________

10. say   _____________   _____________   _____________

B. Using five of the synonyms you chose for the words above, write original sentences for each. Underline the word you chose to use.

1. ____

____

2. ____

____

3. ____

____

4. ____

____

5. ____

____

THE LEGEND OF SLEEPY HOLLOW

Below is a paragraph from a radio play based on *The Legend of Sleepy Hollow.* Read it, paying attention to the underlined words.

The <u>schoolhouse</u> in Sleepy Hollow was ruled over by a <u>man</u> named Ichabod Crane. He was <u>tall</u> and <u>thin</u>, with <u>hands</u> that <u>dangled a mile out of his sleeves</u>, and <u>feet</u> that <u>might have</u> served for shovels. He had <u>huge ears</u>, <u>large glassy-green eyes</u>, and a <u>long nose</u> like a <u>bird's beak</u>. When he <u>walked along on a windy day</u>, one might have taken him for a <u>scarecrow escaped from some cornfield</u>. But inside <u>his own schoolroom</u>, inside the <u>four log walls</u>, he ruled supreme.

A. Write your own version of this paragraph by putting in words of your choice for the underlined words above. Fill in the blanks below and create your own story. Look back at the original paragraph for ideas about the kinds of words used in each blank.

The _______________ in _______________ was ruled over by a _______________

named _______________. He was _______________ and _______________, with

_______________ and _______________ that _______________. He had _______________

_______________, _______________, and a _______________ like a _______________.

When ____, one might have taken

____. But inside _______________, inside

the _______________, he ruled supreme.

B. Draw two pictures below. The first one should be of Ichabod Crane as described in the first paragraph above.

The second picture should be of the person whom you wrote about in the second paragraph above.

No More Forever

Homophones are words that are pronounced the same but have different spellings and meanings. For example:
   Jennie always *wears* her leather jacket to the game.
   The merchant sold his *wares* at a flea market.

way—method of doing something
weigh—to put on a scale

to—toward
too—also; very
two—following one

break—crack or split; damage
brake—device used to slow down

through—by way of
threw—tossed away

peace—freedom from war
piece—part

Some of the homophones above are from "No More Forever." Use the words and definitions to help you complete each sentence below. Write the correct word in each blank space.

   1. Keith pressed hard on the _______________ to stop the car.

   2. Larry ordered a _______________ of pizza.

   3. It is _______________ bad that you cannot come to the picnic with us.

   4. The sun peeked _______________ the clouds.

   5. This year, I _______________ five pounds more than I did last year.

   6. After we go _______________ to the museum, let's go home.

   7. Did you _______________ the window when you hit the ball?

   8. I know an easy _______________ to make a pie.

   9. In only _______________ more days, summer vacation begins.

   10. People all over the world hope for _______________ .

   11. Who _______________ the ball over the fence?

ANNABEL LEE

In "Annabel Lee," Poe uses many words that rhyme. For example, in the first stanza, he rhymes these words:

ago   no   sea   Lee   me

Other rhymes Poe uses in a poem are *love* and *above,* and *side* and *bride.*

A. Think of at least two words to rhyme with each of the following words. Write your choices in the blank spaces. The first one is done for you as an example.

1. day   say   way   play
2. night
3. blue
4. went
5. sit
6. moon
7. sun
8. walk
9. ship
10. rose

B. Choose three pairs of rhyming words. Write a sentence that ends with each to create two-line poems. Here is an example:

see tree

Did you ever want to see
A great big giant apple tree?

1. _______________________________________

2. _______________________________________

3. _______________________________________

Name _______________________________ Date _______________

THE TELL-TALE HEART

In *The Tell-Tale Heart*, Edgar Allan Poe uses many adverbs to help make the meaning of his sentences clear and precise. For example, he writes this sentence:

> Listen! and observe how *clearly*—
>   how *calmly*
> I can tell you the whole story.

The two adverbs italicized above modify the verb *tell*. *Clearly* and *calmly* describe how the narrator will tell the reader the story.

You, too, can write clear, precise sentences with the help of adverbs. Many adverbs end in *-ly*. Some, however, do not.

Here are some examples of adverbs:

Adverbs Modifying Verbs:

> She walked *below*.
> Nicole will arrive *today*.
> The choir sang *beautifully*.

Adverbs Modifying Adjectives:

> She was *very* happy.
> He is *never* wrong.

Adverbs Modifying Adverbs:

> Milton moved *very quickly*.
> Fran arrived *unusually late*.

Here are some adverbs from "The Tell-Tale Heart." Use each one in an original sentence.

1. above ____

____

2. slowly ____

____

3. gradually ____

____

4. gently ____

____

5. cautiously ____

____

6. boldly ____

____

7. soon ____

____

from THE PRAIRIE

A.   Write a sentence using the past tense of each verb below. The sentences should tell about events that took place in *The Prairie*. The first one is done for you as an example.

1.   form _____ The Native Americans formed a circle around Natty Bumppo. _____

2.   sit ____

3.   gaze ____

4.   speak ____

5.   recognize ____

6.   step ____

7.   seem ____

8.   lean ____

9.   request ____

B.   Natty Bumppo's grave has this inscription on it: "May no wanton hand ever disturb his remains." Think of one other possible inscription that could have been placed at the head of the grave. Write it here:

____

____

TO A WATERFOWL

In "To a Waterfowl," many adjectives are used to make the description clear. For example:

<u>falling</u> dew   <u>solitary</u> way

<u>last</u> steps   <u>distant</u> flight

Each of the underlined words describes or modifies a noun.

A. Use each of the adjectives below from "To a Waterfowl" to modify a noun in an original sentence. The first one is done for you as an example.

1. crismson _The crimson sky looked spectacular from the window of the plane._ _______________________________

2. rosy ____

3. cold ____

4. thin ____

5. dark ____

6. boundless ____

B. In "To a Waterfowl," many words rhyme. Write two words to rhyme with each of the words below from that poem.

1. dew   _______________   _______________

2. sky   _______________   _______________

3. wrong   _______________   _______________

4. wide   _______________   _______________

5. care   _______________   _______________

6. end   _______________   _______________

7. flight   _______________   _______________

8. zone   _______________   _______________

A Night *from* Hospital Sketches

Some short sentences can be combined to form longer, more interesting ones. For example, here are two sentences:

The hours I like best are at night.

I was soon promoted to night nurse. These two ideas were combined in "A Night" to form this sentence:

The hours I like best are at night, and so I was soon promoted to night nurse.

By combining the two sentences with the words *and so*, the reader discovers the connection between the two ideas.

Here are some common words used to connect ideas:

and	**so**	**but**	**for**	**or**	**yet**

Choose the best word from the list above to combine each pair of simple sentences below to form a compound sentence. Be sure to put a comma before the connecting word. The first one is done for you as an example.

1. The car broke down.
   The family had to walk six miles.

   _The car broke down, so the family had to walk six miles._______________

2. Yolanda sent me an important letter.
   It still hasn't arrived.

   ____

3. Lucy wants to go to college.
   She will study hard to pass the entrance exam.

   ____

4. The beaches are expected to be clean this summer.
   Many bathers are expected all along the ocean shore.

   ____

5. Wally will go to the library this afternoon.
   He might go to the movies instead.

   ____

6. Quincy waited in line for a ticket to the show.
   All the tickets had already been sold.

   ____

from PAUL REVERE'S RIDE

A.   After each word below from "Paul Revere's Ride," list five more English words that rhyme with it.

1. Revere ____

2. tonight ____

3. sea ____

4. arm ____

5. feet ____

6. magnified ____

7. town ____

8. ride ____

9. boat ____

10. fate ____

B.   Read the following lines from "Paul Revere's Ride." Then write the lines in prose form using ordinary conversational English. Remember: poetic order and rhymes sometimes sound odd in ordinary conversation.

Example: "And I on the opposite shore will be" would be, in conversational English: "I will be on the opposite shore."

1. "Hardly a man is now alive, who remembers that famous day and year."

____

____

2. "Mostly he watched with eager search, the belfry-tower of the old North Church."

____

____

3. "And lo, as he looks on the belfry's height, a glimmer, and then a gleam of light!"

____

____

from THE DAY IS DONE

A. Read the information below. Then complete the chart that follows with information from the reading.

The United States had fewer people in the 1800s than it does now. Until 1920, most people lived on farms.

The nation's first census was conducted in 1790. Philadelphia and New York were the two largest cities. Boston was third—and the biggest in the state of Massachusetts. Boston was always a center of culture. It was the city closest to the mother country, England.

Residents of the East had many more advantages and comforts than those who lived in the West. Some families had lived there for 200 years. Farmers raised their own crops and were able to buy food and goods from other areas. Communication with Europe was easy. The East had many doctors. In the early 1800s, the states in the Northeast were becoming heavily settled. At that time, the Midwest and South were also gaining population.

However, incoming settlers were joining Native Americans on the western frontier when there was much land. Some settlers came to the Northwest by covered wagon. Others walked or went by boat. Distance between places seemed great because of the slowness of transportation. Thus, the West had few cities of any significant size. The Southwest had many Mexicans, largely of Spanish descent. Cowboys raised cattle on large ranches. Many hunted animals for meat. To survive, settlers had to be strong and healthy. People had to be more independent. They had to face many dangers, including hostile Native Americans. The environment was often harsh and dangerous. Water was often scarce, and the weather was unpredictable.

AREA	CITIES	CULTURE	ENVIRONMENT	TYPE OF PEOPLE	FOOD
East					
West					

B. Write a paragraph comparing conditions in the East and the West. Use facts from your completed chart. Tell in which part of the United States you would have preferred to live, in the 1850s.

____

____

____

____

from WALDEN

(This activity includes pages 20–21.)

Use the following information to help answer the questions on page 21.

SOME COMMUNICATIONS AND TRANSPORTATION MILESTONES

These dates tell approximately when important changes in communication and transportation occurred. Notice the increase in inventions that began during the 1800s. Remember that most people could not read and got much of their information by listening to others.

3500 B.C.—First writing (Middle East)

3000 B.C.—Wheel use begins

1500 B.C.—First alphabet (Middle East)

59 B.C.—First newspaper (posted on Roman walls)

A.D. 105—Paper invented

1045—Movable type invented (China)

1100—Europe starts using wagons

1400—Carriages first used

1436—Europe discovers movable type; book printing starts (Germany)

1490s—Transoceanic voyages become fairly common

Mid-1500s—Pencil invented (England)

1600s—First real printed newspapers (Holland)

1811—First steam-powered printing press, ships

1826—First photograph (France)

1830—First railroads (England)

1840—Railroads become common (U.S., Europe)

1862—First trans-continental telegraph (U.S.)

1866—First transatlantic telegraph cable

1873—First commercial typewriters (U.S.)

1876—First telephone (U.S.)

1877—First phonograph (U.S.)

1890s—First pictures in newspapers

1890—First automobiles (France, Germany)

1890—First wireless telegraph

1903—First airplane (U.S.)

1920—First radio broadcast (U.S.)

1936—First TV broadcast (England)

1950s—First jet airplanes (Europe)

1955—First videotapes (U.S.)

1957—First commercial computers introduced (U.S.)

1957—First space satellite launched (USSR)

1960—First photocopying (U.S.)

from WALDEN

(Continued from page 20.)

A. Use the information on page 20 to answer these questions.

1. How could educated Americans in cities get their news and opinions in 1850?

____

____

2. More than half of all Americans were illiterate until the U.S. Civil War (1861–65). What methods could they use to get their information?

____

____

3. In the 1800s, the mass media (ways of communicating to many people at once) were mostly printed (see question 1). What new media do we have today?

____

____

4. How did people travel over long distances in the early part of the 1800s?

____

____

B. Answer these questions about communications and transportation, based on the information given in the chart on page 20.

1. About how long have people been using the wheel?

____

2. What types of transportation use wheels? _______________________

____

3. What kinds of communication use paper? _______________________

____

4. Which kinds of communication do you use most? _______________________

5. Which kinds of transportation do you use most? _______________________

from WALDEN

Synonyms are words that have the same or almost the same meaning.
Big and *large* are synonyms. **Antonym**s are words that have opposite
meanings. *Big* and *small* are antonyms.

**Match the following words from *Walden* with a synonym and an antonym from the
lists below. Put the letter for the synonyms in the first blank and the letter for the
antonyms in the second. You can use a dictionary or thesaurus to help you.**

SYN.	ANT.	WORD	SYNONYM	ANTONYM
_______	_______	**1.** surveyed (verb)	**a.** pay	**q.** complexity
_______	_______	**2.** radiated (verb)	**b.** hungrily	**r.** happiness
_______	_______	**3.** surpassed (verb)	**c.** regarded	**s.** generously
_______	_______	**4.** dilapidated (adj.)	**d.** run-down	**t.** ignored
_______	_______	**5.** compensation (noun)	**e.** misery	**u.** penalty
_______	_______	**6.** plentiful (adj.)	**f.** spread out	**v.** well-kept
_______	_______	**7.** greedily (adv.)	**g.** plainness	**w.** centered
_______	_______	**8.** dejection (noun)	**h.** sadness	**x.** scarce
_______	_______	**9.** wretchedness (noun)	**i.** exceeded	**y.** joy
_______	_______	**10.** simplicity (noun)	**j.** fruitful	**z.** lagged

from NATURE

A.   Adjectives are descriptive words that help to create images for the reader. Think of adjectives that might describe a person you know. Fill in the chart below.

	OVERALL APPEAR-ANCE	PERSONAL STYLE	TEMPERA-MENT	VOICE	HAIR
Example:	Tall and thin Beautiful Large blue eyes	Graceful Gestures a lot	Always happy Smiles a lot	Soft and low	Black and straight Long To her shoulders
A relative					
A male friend					
A female friend					

B.   Write a paragraph describing a person. Use the adjectives that you developed above.

____

____

____

____

____

____

DAVID SWAN

A. The following selection is from "David Swan." Identify the parts of speech of the numbered words. You may refer to the list of parts of speech below to help you. The first one has been done for you.

PARTS OF SPEECH

Noun	Pronoun
Verb	Proper noun
Adjective	Article
Adverb	Preposition

```
 1   2     3     4                        5
We  find  David , at  the age of 20, on the high

                                   6
road to the city of Boston, where an uncle

 7              8    9
was to take him behind the counter in his

          10
grocery store.
```

1. __________ pronoun __________
2. _______________________________
3. _______________________________
4. _______________________________
5. _______________________________
6. _______________________________
7. _______________________________
8. _______________________________
9. _______________________________
10. ______________________________

B. Read the information below. Then fill in the chart that follows. One comparison has been done as an example.

The first American supermarket was founded in Chicago in 1931. Before that, there were smaller individual grocery stores, including the famous country stores, which served a territory for miles around. List some ways the markets of 100 years ago—like David Swan's—might have been different from the markets of today. What do today's markets have that old-time markets did not?

YESTERDAY'S MARKETS

Fairly small, run by their owner

____

____

____

____

____

TODAY'S MARKETS

Much larger—supermarkets

____

____

____

____

____

Name _______________________ *Date* _______________________

I'M NOBODY/A WORD/I NEVER SAW A MOOR/
THE SKY IS LOW/SOME KEEP THE SABBATH/
LETTER TO THOMAS WENTWORTH HIGGINSON

A. Review the definitions of the figures of speech: metaphor, simile, personification, and onomatopoeia. Write them in the space below.

1. Simile: ____

____

2. Metaphor: ____

____

3. Personification: _______________________________________

____

4. Onomatopoeia: ____

____

B. Choose a *natural* event common in the area where you live—a thunderstorm, windstorm, forest fire, hurricane, tornado, snowstorm, tidal wave, sunny day in the woods or mountains or at the beach, earthquake, etc. Develop figures of speech for each natural event.
For instance:
Metaphor: The wind was a bulldozer, knocking down everything.
Simile: A windstorm is like a giant sneezing.
Personification: The giant called Wind sneezed and blew away the town.
Onomatopoeia: The wind whooshed away everything in its path.

Natural event: ____

1. Simile: ____

2. Metaphor: ____

3. Personification: _______________________________________

4. Onomatopoeia: ____

I'M NOBODY/A WORD/I NEVER SAW A MOOR/
THE SKY IS LOW/SOME KEEP THE SABBATH/
LETTER TO THOMAS WENTWORTH HIGGINSON

A. When Emily Dickinson talks about a "nobody" in her poem, she seems to mean a person who is not well-known. Do you agree? How would you define "nobody"? Write your definition here.

____

____

____

B. The opposite of "nobody" is "somebody." Using Emily Dickinson's ideas and your own, write a definition of "somebody."

____

____

____

C. Name three people or types of people that the American culture defines as "somebody" and briefly tell why each is considered "somebody." An example is given.

PERSON	WHY?
President of the United States	Elected by people, represents everybody
_________________________	_________________________
_________________________	_________________________
_________________________	_________________________

D. Name three people in your native country considered to be "somebody" and then tell why they are considered "somebody."

____

____

____

____

I'm nobody/A word/I never saw a Moor/ The sky is low/Some keep the Sabbath/ Letter to Thomas Wentworth Higginson

Metaphor—compares two unlike things, without using extra words: My love is a red, red rose.

Simile—compares two unlike objects using the word *like* or *as*: He is *like* a frog.

Personification—gives human characteristics to a nonhuman force or object: A traveling flake of snow debates whether it will go.

Hyperbole—an exaggerated statement for poetic effect: The *whole world* was lit by tiny fireflies.

Alliteration—the repetition of initial consonant sounds within a sentence or line of poetry: Peter Piper picked a peck of pickled peppers.

Onomatopoeia—the use of words that sound like their meaning: The saw *buzzed* loudly.

A. Study the above definitions. Fill in the following blanks:

1. "Sally sells seashells by the seashore" uses what kinds of sounds? ________________

2. Create a metaphor that begins, "The wind is ________________________"

3. Create a simile that begins, "The wind is ________________________"

4. Create a personification that begins, "The wind is ________________________"

5. Create a hyperbole that begins, "The wind is ________________________"

6. Create an onomatopoeia that begins, "Tom tells ________________________"

B. "Somebody" and "nobody" are opposites, or antonyms. Write an antonym for each of the following words from Emily Dickinson's poems.

1. day ____

2. public ____

3. never ____

4. low ____

5. narrow ____

THE FIRST SNOWFALL

POETIC TERMS

a. onomatopoeia

b. metaphor

c. simile

d. hyperbole

e. personification

f. alliteration

A. Below are definitions of poetic terms. Match each term to its definition by writing the correct letter on the blank.

_______ **1.** Comparison using *like* or *as*

_______ **2.** Comparison saying that one thing *is* another

_______ **3.** Comparison giving life to nonhuman objects

_______ **4.** An exaggerated comparison

_______ **5.** Words that sound like their meanings

_______ **6.** Repetition of initial sounds in a poem

B. Read the following quotes from "The First Snowfall" and decide which type(s) of figurative language or sound device are being used. Your choices are simile, metaphor, personification, hyperbole, onomatopoeia, and alliteration.

1. And the sudden fluries of snowbirds,
   Like brown leaves whirling by

____

2. When that mound was heaped so high.

____

3. I remembered the gradual patience
   That fell from that cloud like snow.

____

4. Every pine and fir and hemlock
   Wore ermine too dear for an earl

____

5. The stiff rails softened to swan's-down
   And still fluttered down the snow

____

from MOBY-DICK

A. Identify the following story elements in *Moby-Dick*.

1. Setting (place where story happens) _______________________________

2. Protagonist(s) (the heroes—good guys) _______________________________

3. Antagonist(s) (the villains—bad guys) _______________________________

4. Conflict (Is there more than one?): Man vs. Man, Nature, Society, Self

____

5. Rising action (the author creates a problem to be solved) occurs when?

____

6. Falling action (the problem is being solved) occurs when?

____

7. Climax (solution of the problem) _______________________________

____

8. Dénouement (events that happen after the climax) _______________________

____

____

____

B.   Here are some words that come from other languages. From which language did they come? Use your dictionary to help you find the answer. Write the meaning of each word along with its country of origin. The first word has been done as an example.

		FOREIGN LANGUAGE	MEANING
1.	siesta	Spanish	Afternoon nap
2.	igloo		
3.	shawl		
4.	goulash		
5.	ranch		
6.	picturesque		
7.	typhoon		
8.	bronco		

SONG OF SLAVES IN THE DESERT

A.   The following sentences summarize each of the five stanzas of "Song of Slaves in the Desert." Determine which stanza matches which summary sentence and arrange them in the order in which the author wrote them. Number them in the blanks. For example, the first stanza of the poem is best summarized by sentence *c*: "The slaves wonder where they are going." So put a *1* (for first stanza) in the blank. Do the same with the other sentences.

________   **a.**   The slaves recalled their green homeland as they went through a strange new country.

________   **b.**   They prayed to their god to take care of them.

________   **c.**   The slaves wondered where they were going.

________   **d.**   As the slaves moved from their home country, the hot desert trip was very hard for them.

________   **e.**   While on the long journey, many of the slaves died.

B.   On the lines below, write a paragraph in which you use the summary sentences in their correct order as you have numbered them above. Add some supporting details.

____

____

____

____

____

____

____

____

____

____

____

____

____

SONG OF SLAVES IN THE DESERT

A. Make a list of five adjectives (descriptive words) that describe the sights, sounds, feelings, tastes, and smells of (a) the place where you live now; (b) the larger area around your home.

For example, you might describe your house in terms of *sight* as being *tan* with *blue* trim, *wide, attractive,* with *tall green* trees in front, *one-story,* etc. If it is an apartment, it might be described in terms of being *three-story, tall, narrow, massive, redbrick* with *green* shutters, or whatever it looks like.

Then write sounds, feel (touching sensations), tastes, and smells you associate with your home and the surrounding area.

ADJECTIVES FOR YOUR HOME NOW:

1. Sight ____

____

2. Sound ____

____

3. Feel ____

____

4. Taste ____

____

5. Smell ____

B. Write a brief paragraph about your home now, using the words you listed above.

____

____

____

____

____

____

____

____

____

I Hear America Singing/
O Captain! My Captain!/
When I Heard the Learn'd Astronomer

Symbols are people, objects, or things that represent or stand for something else. The American flag, for instance, stands for the United States. So does the American eagle. Red, white, and blue are colors that stand for the United States. So does a tall, thin man with a white beard who wears those colors on his suit. ("Uncle Sam" is a fictional "mascot" often used to represent the country.) In Walt Whitman's poem "O Captain! My Captain!", the poet uses many symbols, among them, the captain and the ship.

Countries have symbols, such as flags. Most schools have symbols, too—nicknames, colors, mascots, and other objects and ideas.

A.   List symbols of your school below, and those of two other schools or colleges that you know. Follow the example.

SCHOOL NAME	COLORS	NICKNAME	MASCOT	OTHER SYMBOLS
University of Nebraska	Red and White	Cornhuskers Huskers	Farmer in straw hat ("Big Red")	Ear of corn
Your high school				
Another high school				
Another college				

B.   Now compare notes with your classmates from other countries. List flag colors, symbols, and people associated with their home countries.

COUNTRY NAME	FLAG COLORS	SYMBOLS	FAMOUS PEOPLE
France	Blue, white, red	Eiffel Tower, berets, croissants	Napoleon Joan of Arc

I Hear America Singing/
O Captain! My Captain!/
When I Heard the Learn'd Astronomer

Read the information below. Then complete the sentences that follow.

Americans created many inventions during the 1800s. These changed life greatly. In 1880, for instance, trains for the first time went at amazing speed—100 miles an hour. Other new methods of transport were the bicycle, the steamboat, the zeppelin, and the automobile. (By 1938, the fastest speed was 400 m.p.h. Today, Earth satellites travel 16,000 miles an hour—and faster to get into outer space.)

Many other inventions changed the way people worked. During the 1800s, these inventions appeared: automatic reaper (for cutting grain), gas refrigeration, cameras, the telegraph, sewing machines, dynamite, typewriters, telephones, phonographs, electric lights, skyscrapers, zippers, matches, X-ray machines, stethoscopes, and the radio. New tools allowed oil drilling. This, in turn, made possible the car and the motorcycle.

Walt Whitman wrote about some changing jobs in his poem "I Hear America Singing." Most of them were men's jobs. Most women were still working at home, as wives and mothers. However, some did small jobs or "piecework" in their homes.

1. The new _______________ of the 19th century changed life greatly.

2. Before 1880, people had not gone more than _______________ miles per hour. The new invention that could go this fast was the _______________ .

3. Other new methods of transportation in the 1800s were the _______________ ,
    _______________ , _______________ , and _______________ .

4. While today, _______________ travel 16,000 miles per hour, and faster to get into outerspace, back in 1938, _______________ m.p.h. was the fastest speed.

5. Farmers' lives became easier due to the invention of the _______________
    _______________ .

6. Communication became easier because of the invention of the _______________
    and the _______________ .

7. Candles and lanterns became less important because the _______________ was invented.

8. In Whitman's poem "I Hear America Singing," what jobs for women are listed?
    _______________ _______________ , and _______________ .

I Hear America Singing/
O Captain! My Captain!/
When I Heard the Learn'd Astronomer

Read the information below.

The inventions (of the 19th century) caused many changes in American life. Many new jobs were created. More people started working in large factories. Labor unions began. Because of their clothes, factory workers came to be called "blue-collar workers." People who worked in offices and management were called "white-collar workers."

In 1860, the prices of goods were less than one-tenth of what they are today. Salaries bought even less. People had more children, and most women were homemakers. Most people lived on farms. There, bad weather often ruined or damaged the family's food supply. Life was hard.

Until the Civil War, most people could not read or write. On the Western Frontier, schools were often far apart. Many children had to walk long distances. High schools were not common, and people married young. Young men started to work as teenagers. They often dropped out of school to help their families. Children sometimes had jobs at the ages of seven or eight. No child labor laws protected children then.

Health care was not very advanced. People lived to an average age of forty-five as late as 1900. Many children died of childhood diseases. In the first half of the 19th century, some people were killed by Native Americans.

Still, many new inventions greatly changed life. Life improved for everyone.

Fill in the blanks to complete the following sentences. The first one is done for you.

1. New inventions greatly changed American life and created many new ______jobs______ . Large ______factories______ became places where more people worked.

2. Factory workers were called ____________ ____________ workers, while those who worked in officers were given the name ____________ ____________ workers.

3. Prices today are more than ____________ times as high as in 1860.

4. In 1860, salaries bought ____________ .

5. Most women worked as ____________ , and people married ____________ .

6. Most people lived on ____________ , and food was often damaged by poor ____________ .

Name ____ Date ___________________

THE GIFT OF THE MAGI

A sentence has a subject and a verb. Sentences do not begin with a conjunction, such as *but* or *and*. Sometimes, for special effect, writers use phrases called sentence fragments. These are phrases that are punctuated like sentences, but they are only groups of words.

Fragments in O. Henry's "The Gift of the Magi" include most of the first paragraph.

The opening has no verb: "One dollar and eighty-seven cents."

It is followed by a short, complete sentence, "That was all." It has a subject (*that*) and a verb (*was*).

Then another fragment follows, "And sixty cents of it was in pennies." Complete sentences do not begin with *and*.

The next phrase has many words, but it is still a fragment.

Then comes "One dollar and eighty-seven cents"—again. It has no verb.

"And the next day was Christmas," is not a sentence. It begins with *and*.

A long phrase at the end of the second paragraph says: "Which instigates the reflection that life is made up of three stages—snobs, sniffles, and smiles, with sniffles in the lead." Though this is a long phrase, it is not a complete sentence. The subject should be a noun or pronoun, and *which* is neither. A similar example occurs at the end of the fourth paragraph: "Which is all very good."

Working with a partner, decide which statements are fragments (F) and which are complete sentences (S). Add whatever words are necessary to make each fragment a complete sentence.

________   **1.** Expenses had been greater than she had planned. _______________________

________   **2.** They always are. ____

________   **3.** Only one dollar to buy a present for Jim. _______________________

________   **4.** Her Jim. ____

________   **5.** Going to the store. ____

________   **6.** She was on her way to the store. ________________________________

________   **7.** Come to the party. ____

________   **8.** The team's playing the game. ____________________________________

________   **9.** And she went into the store. ____________________________________

________   **10.** But I didn't mean it! ____

________   **11.** Seventeen movies and twelve books. ____________________________

________   **12.** That was great! ____

Name ____   Date _______________________

THE GIFT OF THE MAGI

English and other languages contain idioms. An **idiom** is a phrase or expression whose meaning cannot be understood from the usual meanings of the words. *It is raining cats and dogs* is an idiom. It means that it is raining very hard, not that cats and dogs are actually falling from the sky. Another example of an idiom is *Hold your tongue.* This means to keep quiet, not literally grab your tongue with your fingers.

Different kinds of writing use different kinds of English, called formal, informal, and colloquial. O. Henry used an interesting combination of all three types.

•**Formal,** or literary, English uses more longer or "grown-up" words. It is used for formal reports, important papers, ceremonies, and special occasions. The writing sounds flowery. It can also sound stilted or forced. Here is an example of formal English: "We are assembled tonight to bid farewell to Sam, as he retires after 25 years of dedicated service to the company."

•**Informal** English is used when ordinary people talk to each other. Most newspapers and magazines use informal language; so do most movies and television shows. Informal words tend to be shorter than formal ones. Here is an example of informal English: "Tonight we are saying good-bye to Sam, who has worked with us for 25 years."

•**Colloquial** English, or **slang**, is very informal. Sometimes, it is not grammatical. Colloquial language is lively and expressive, and it changes very quickly. *Awesome*, a slang word used frequently today, may be out of date next year. Here is an example of colloquial English: "Our buddy Sam finally made it to retirement. We'll sure miss him. See you, big fella."

Working with a partner, decide whether the words below are formal (F), informal (I), or colloquial (C) English. Remember that slang is considered colloquial English.

1. How do you do? ______ Hello. ______ Hi. ______

2. I am commencing my journey. ______ I'm taking off. ______ I'm starting my trip. ______

3. Let's grab a bite. ______ Let's eat some food. ______ Shall we dine? ______

4. He became angry. ______ He got mad. ______ He blew his cool. ______

5. She is attractive. ______ She's pretty. ______ She's as cute as a button. ______

6. He was not interested. ______ He didn't care. ______ He wasn't tuned in. ______

7. Cool it! ______ Stay calm! ______ Don't get worked up! ______

8. Let's party! ______ Shall we go and have a good time? ______ Let's have some fun! ______

THE GIFT OF THE MAGI

A. With a partner or group, make a list of gift-giving times in the United States and in other countries. What kinds of gifts are given on which holidays?

COUNTRY	NAME OF HOLIDAY	IT CELEBRATES	GIFTS GIVEN TO WHOM
United States	Birthday	Individual's birthday	The individual from family and friends

B. Answer the following questions after discussing your list with your partner or a group.

1. Could the situation in "The Gift of the Magi" happen to people in the United States today? Yes or no? _______________ Why or why not?

____

____

2. Can you think of a gift-giving situation like that in "The Gift of the Magi" that could occur today? Explain.

____

____

____

THE REVOLT OF MOTHER

Dialect is language used by people in a particular place or group. The pronunciation, vocabulary, and sentence structure in dialect are different from informal English. Mark Twain writes, "Friends of yourn?" meaning, "Are they friends of yours?" and Langston Hughes writes, "Life for me ain't been no crystal stair."

Write the following dialect as standard English.

1. He *done* no good. ________________________________

   ____

2. Where *was* you *goin'*? ________________________________

   ____

3. What is you *diggin' fer*? ________________________________

   ____

4. Who *is* you *lookin' fer*? ________________________________

   ____

5. I can't leave this wood *nohow*. ________________________________

   ____

6. I *is s'posed* to see you in *jest* a minute. ________________________________

   ____

7. I *wants* to *git* there *afore* two o'clock. ________________________________

   ____

8. I *ain't* got *nothing* to say about it. ________________________________

   ____

9. There *wa'n't never nothin'* there. ________________________________

   ____

10. Come *set* beside me for a *spell*. ________________________________

Name ____ Date _______________

THE REVOLT OF MOTHER

Review the many literary elements used in fiction. Remember that fiction is a story about imaginary characters and events. Types of fiction include novels (longer stories), short stories, and plays.

Match the literary elements with examples from "The Revolt of Mother."

a. *Setting*—where and when a story occurs

b. *Character*—a person in a story. His or her problems form the basis of the action.

c. *Plot*—what happens in the story, the action

d. *Foreshadowing*—events in a story that offer clues to the ending

e. *Rising action*—events that lead up to the climax

f. *Conflict*—Man vs. Man, Nature, Self, Society, Machine, Unknown

g. *Theme*—the message, what the story is trying to say

h. *Tone*—the author's attitude toward the subject matter

i. *Imagery and figurative language*— mental picture that appeals to the emotions and five senses

j. *Metaphor*—comparison saying one thing is another

k. *Simile*—comparison using the word *like* or *as*

l. *Symbolism*—using symbols, one thing to represent another

_______ **1.** Father against Mother

_______ **2.** A man and a woman argue about how to use a new farm building.

_______ **3.** Father leaves town, and Mother moves the family into the new barn.

_______ **4.** The children predict Mother will move everyone into the barn.

_______ **5.** Mother

_______ **6.** On a farm during the late 1800s

_______ **7.** The barn *stands* for Mother's desire to be consulted on the farm business.

_______ **8.** A woman wins a battle with her husband about how to use the barn.

_______ **9.** Comparison that says "Opportunities *are* the guideposts of the Lord."

_______ **10.** The story is told seriously, talking about Mother's feelings.

_______ **11.** Comparison that says, "A fragrance *like* warm honey came into the room."

_______ **12.** The author describes how the new barn looks.

THE REVOLT OF MOTHER

An **epilogue** is a closing section added onto a story. It often offers further comment, interpretation, or information related to the story.

A. In a group, discuss how the relationship between Mother and Father in "The Revolt of Mother" changes during the story. Write the change.

1. What change occurred in Mother's attitude? _______________________________

2. What change occurred in Father's attitude? _______________________________

3. What change occurred in Mother's actions? _______________________________

4. What change occurred in Father's actions? _______________________________

5. Did you like the change in Mother? _____________ In Father? _____________

   Why? ____

   ____

6. What might happen a year after these events occurred—and the daughter has been married? How might the characters act then?

   ____

   ____

   ____

B. The women's movement of the 1960s brought about a change in American thinking. It offered the idea that men and women should be equal partners and have equal opportunities. Answer the following questions about the women's movement and the story.

1. Was Mother a believer in the women's movement? Explain your answer with examples from the story. ____

   ____

   ____

2. Do you agree or disagree with the women's movement? _____________________

   Why? ____

   ____

3. What is the attitude of your parents or adult family members toward the women's movement?

   ____

Name _______________________________   *Date* _______________________

HOW TO TELL A STORY

A. Fill in the letter to match each term on the left with a description on the right.

Kinds of Discourse

a. *Exposition*—presenting information

b. *Narrative*—telling a story

c. *Description*—describing something

d. *Persuasion*—arguing for a viewpoint

______ **1.** One kind of discourse tells what something looks like.

______ **2.** Another kind of discourse offers information.

______ **3.** Still another type of discourse tries to persuade people to a viewpoint.

______ **4.** The fourth variety of discourse presents a story.

B. Fill in the letter to match each term on the right to a kind of exposition described on the left.

______ **1.** This kind of exposition explains differences between things.

______ **2.** Another type of exposition explains likenesses between things.

______ **3.** One variety of exposition looks at the parts of things and how they operate or what they mean.

______ **4.** A fourth kind of exposition explains what a thing is and shows its purpose.

______ **5.** This type of exposition puts something in classes of things like it.

Methods of Exposition

a. *Defining*—telling what it is and showing its purpose

b. *Comparing*—telling how two or more things are alike

c. *Contrasting*—telling how two or more things are different

d. *Classifying*—putting it in a class of other things similar to it

e. *Analyzing*—discussing its parts and what they do or mean

C. With a partner, create an interview with Mark Twain. Reread "How to Tell a Story" and the biography of Twain in your textbook. Write the questions and answers on a separate sheet of paper.

HOW TO TELL A STORY

Humor is something that is funny and makes us smile or laugh. However, writers use humor to do more than that.

Humor often uses exaggeration to describe situations and people's actions and feelings. The hope is that by making people "larger than life," their personalities will be more obvious. Readers may learn things about the characters—and themselves—that they might not realize from a serious piece of writing.

Two of the best and best-known humorists are Mark Twain and James Thurber. Twain made fun of 19th-century American society. He hoped that behind the humor people would recognize their pretensions and prejudices and work to overcome them, making the world a better place for all. Thurber, on the other hand, concentrated on individual people (and animals) and the zany things they do, say, and think. He hoped his readers would appreciate the lighter side of their personality and not take themselves so seriously.

A type of humor often used in literature is irony. This technique involves surprising, interesting, or amusing contradictions. Irony often involves a so-called surprise ending, such as in O. Henry's story "The Gift of the Magi."

Humor helps us feel better. It relieves our tensions. At its best, it makes us see things in new and deeper ways. Even when humor has a serious purpose, it is fun.

Fill in blanks with information from the selection above:

1. Humor is _______________ and makes us _______________.

2. Humorous writing often uses _______________ to describe people and situations.

3. A writer of humor is called a _______________.

4. Two famous humorists are _______________ and _______________.

5. Twain made fun of American _______________.

6. Thurber made fun of _______________.

7. _______________ is a type of humor often used in literature.

8. Irony involves surprising or amusing _______________.

9. A type of irony used by O. Henry is called _______________ _______________.

10. Humor relieves our _______________.

11. Humor is _______________.

TO BUILD A FIRE

Every story has a **setting**. That is, it takes place somewhere, at some time. Sometimes the setting occurs at a very specific place. That could be in a particular home in a particular city. It could be the White House, the President's residence in Washington, DC. The story "To Build a Fire" takes place in northern Canada, near the Alaskan border. It happened during the gold Rush days, about 1900.

The **theme** of the story deals with a young man who does not take advice from older, wiser miners. He does not realize how very cold the weather there can be. He travels alone, believing he can handle any situation. He is wrong. The young man makes some mistakes, and he pays with his life.

In this story, fate or luck played a cruel trick on the young man. He fell into the water and could not dry out before he froze to death.

With a group, discuss the following questions.

1. Which is more important in this story—time or place? Why?

   ____

2. If the setting, the time, the place or both were changed, would it have an important effect on the story? Explain.

   ____

   ____

   ____

   ____

3. There is an old saying: "There are three kinds of people in the world: Happy ones, who learn from the experience of others; wise ones, who learn from their own experience; and fools, who learn from neither." Do you think this saying applies to "To Build a Fire?" Is the young man happy, wise, or foolish. Use details from the story to support your answer.

   ____

   ____

   ____

   ____

TO BUILD A FIRE

In "To Build a Fire," at least eight words from the native Inuit or Eskimo culture were used. They became familiar to Americans partly because they were in this story.

Four of those words relate to keeping warm:

- *Anorak*—a heavy jacket with a hood.
- *Igloo*—an Eskimo house or hut built from blocks of packed snow, usually dome-shaped.
- *Mukluk*—an Eskimo boot, made of sealskin or reindeer skin.
- *Parka*—a hip-length pullover fur garment with a hood.

The other four relate to transportation:

- *Husky*—a strong dog used to pull sleds in the North.
- *Malamute*—a breed of large, strong dogs with thick coats. Malamutes are gray or black-and-white with bushy tails.
- *Kayak*—an Eskimo canoe made of skins stretched over a wood frame. It is covered completely, except for an opening for the boat's occupant in the center.
- *Uniak*—a large open boat of skins stretched over a wood frame. Used to transport goods, it is traditionally rowed by women.

A. Use four Inuit words in sentences of your own.

1. ____

2. ____

3. ____

4. ____

B. Make a list of foreign words that have entered the English language. Compare your words with the words of other students in your class.

	WORD	COUNTRY	MEANING
1.	__________	__________	__________
2.	__________	__________	__________
3.	__________	__________	__________
4.	__________	__________	__________

C. Now use the words you listed above in original sentences.

1. ____

2. ____

3. ____

4. ____

Name ____   **Date** _______________________

America the Beautiful

Katherine Lee Bates's poem, "America the Beautiful" contains references to many parts of the United States. It also refers to historic events. The poem offers some major images associated with the United States. Here are some that refer to states or sections of the nation.

Match these ideas with letters of images from the right.

_______ **1.** A nation bounded by waters

_______ **2.** Colorful mountain views

_______ **3.** Wide-open country

_______ **4.** Settlers find their own new land

_______ **5.** Wheat, corn, rye, maize, and so forth

_______ **6.** Apples, peaches, plums, and so forth

_______ **7.** Skyscrapers rise from the plains.

_______ **8.** Americans gain independence in war.

_______ **9.** Early American leaders planned great things.

_______ **10.** Early leaders had high hopes for the future of America.

_______ **11.** A precious metal means "the best."

_______ **12.** Brotherhood is an American belief.

a. *Spacious skies*—refers to Midwestern and Western states where views of the sky and nature are not blocked by cities.

b. *Amber waves of grain*—any farming areas that grow wheat or similar crops.

c. *From purple mountain majesties*—either the Rocky Mountains in the West or the Appalacians in the East.

d. *The fruited plain*—lands where much fruit and/or vegetables are grown.

e. *From sea to shining sea*—from ocean to ocean.

f. *Beautiful for Pilgrim feet*—refers to settlement of the new land (Massachusetts) by the Pilgrims.

g. *In liberating strife*—refers to the Revolutionary War, which liberated America from England.

h. *May God thy gold refine*—probably refers to gold in the ground and use of the word *gold* to mean "the best."

i. *Oh beautiful for patriot dream*—the hopes and dreams of the founding fathers were beautiful.

j. *That sees beyond the years*—the founding fathers developed plans that lasted many years.

k. *Thine alabaster cities gleam*—the cities' large buildings shine from a distance.

l. *And crown they good with brotherhood*—The American ideal is brotherhood.

AMERICA THE BEAUTIFUL

A. Complete the chart below with features and characteristics of a state of your choice. Use the information about Alaska as a guide, but include more features.

STATE	FEATURES AND CHARACTERISTICS
Alaska	Very cold weather—down to 80° below; snow; mountains

B. Write an image for each statement in your chart.

____

____

____

C. A *synonym* is a word that means the same or nearly the same as another word. Write a synonym for each of these words from "America the Beautiful." You may use a dictionary or thesaurus.

1. spacious _______________________ **3.** flaw _______________________

2. mend _______________________ **4.** wilderness _______________________

AMERICA THE BEAUTIFUL

A. Answer the following questions.

1. Write some images of your state or native country that have left a lasting impression on your mind. Make them as vivid as possible.

____

____

2. Compare images with other members of your group. Try to help others express their images in a way you understand.

3. Write rhyming words for the images you have created. If you cannot think of any rhymes, ask your group members for help.

____

____

4. Write four two-line poems using the images and the rhyming words.

____

____

____

____

____

____

____

____

B. Illustrate one of your poems in the space below.

BARTER/THE FALLING STAR/THE LONG HILL/
I SHALL NOT CARE

In this unit, there are poems with several different rhyme schemes. In "The Falling Star," the rhyme scheme is aabbcc. This means that lines 1 and 2 rhyme (a); lines 3 and 4 rhyme (b); and lines 5 and 6 rhyme (c).

In "Barter," the rhyme scheme is abcbdd. This means that line 1 is (a); the last word rhymes with no other line. Line 2 is (b); and its last word rhymes with line 4. Line 3 is (c); its last word rhymes with no other line. Lines 5 and 6 are (d); the last words rhyme with each other.

A. Use your textbook to determine the rhyme schemes for the two other Teasdale poems and for the other poems in this unit.

1. "The Long Hill" by Teasdale _______________

2. "I Shall Not Care" by Teasdale _______________

3. "America the Beautiful" by Bates _______________

4. "Richard Cory" by Robinson _______________

5. "O Captain! My Captain!" by Whitman _______________

B. Most poems have basic themes—idea or moods that they try to express. Teasdale's poems express her feelings at different times in her life. The themes and moods are quite different. The selections start with a very happy poem and end with a very sad one. Discuss each of the four poems in pairs. Find the basic message of each.

1. "Barter" _______________________________________

2. "The Falling Star" _______________________________________

3. "The Long Hill" _______________________________________

4. "I Shall Not Care" _______________________________________

RICHARD CORY

Several selections in this unit involve irony. **Irony** happens when the results of a situation are the opposite of those expected. Stories often have ironic endings. For instance, it is ironic that the same author wrote both the first poem, "Barter" and then later, the fourth poem, "I Shall Not Care." "Barter" was written when she felt great joy in the beauty of living. "I Shall Not Care" expresses total despair; the author feels ready for death.

A. What is ironic in each of these poems and stories?

1. "Richard Cory" ____

____

2. "To Build a Fire" ____

____

3. "The Gift of the Magi" _____________________________________

____

4. "The Revolt of Mother" _____________________________________

____

The beginning of Charles Dickens's novel, *The Tale of Two Cities* states:

It was the best of times, it was the worst of times, it was the age of wisdom, it was the age of foolishness, it was the epoch of belief, it was the epoch of incredulity, it was the season of Light, it was the season of Darkness, it was the spring of hope, it was the winter of despair.

B. What Dickens is suggesting is that contradictory and ironic things often go on at the same time. Some things are good and some are bad at the same time—in the United States and many other countries. In the modern world, what is ironic about the following conditions?

1. War and peace

____

____

2. Homelessness and wealth

____

____

RICHARD CORY

The poem "Richard Cory" uses many vivid words. *Vivid* means "lively" or "producing a strong impression on your senses." The poem says, for instance that he "fluttered pulses" when he talked. This means that he made the ladies' hearts start to beat faster; he was a very attractive man.

Note the vivid terms in quotation marks below. Tell what each term means. The first one has been done for you.

1. He "fluttered pulses" when he talked He made the ladies' hearts beat faster; he was an attractive man.

2. He was a gentleman from "sole to crown." _______________________________

3. He was always "quietly arrayed." _______________________________

4. He "glittered" when he walked. _______________________________

5. He was "schooled" in every grace. _______________________________

6. We went without the meat and "cursed" the bread. _______________________________

Name _______________________________________ *Date* _______________

A Day's Wait

A. In column A, write an example for the situation. In column B, write what someone might say to show courage in that situation. In column C, write how the person might show courage through his or her actions.

A	COURAGEOUS REACTION	
	B **WORDS**	**C** **ACTIONS**
ILLNESS Example: the flu	I'll take the medicine.	Determined, unsmiling
PAIN		
DISAPPOINT- MENT		
FRIGHT		
FAILURE		
NEW SITUATION		

B. Use the information in the chart to describe a courageous person. Write your paragraph on a separate sheet of paper.

A Day's Wait

A. Use the words from the box to complete the sentences from "A Day's Wait."

shivering	sick	headache	white	dark areas
ached	white-faced	flushed	fever	miserable

1. He was _______________, his face was white, and he walked as though it _______________ to move.

2. "I've got a _______________."

3. But when I came downstairs he was dressed, sitting by the fire, looking a very sick and _______________ boy of nine years.

4. When I put my hand on his forehead I knew he had a _______________.

5. "You go up to bed," I said, "you're _______________."

6. His face was very_______________ and there were _______________ under his eyes.

7. I went up to him and found him in exactly the position I had left him, _______________ but with the tops of his cheeks _______________ by the fever, sitting still, as he stared at the foot of the bed.

B. Using some of the words above, write a short paragraph describing a time when you were ill. Draw a picture of yourself ailing on the right.

____

____

____

____

____

____

____

____

____

____

LAMENT/AFTERNOON ON A HILL

A. Fill in the missing consonants to complete these words from the two poems by Edna St. Vincent Millay in your textbook.

1. _______ ather

2. _______ edicine

3. _______ ants

4. _______ undred

5. _______ oise

6. _______ eys

7. _______ ook

8. _______ uiet

9. _______ obacco

10. _______ ackets

B. Fill in the blanks with consonant blends to complete the words.

CONSONANT BLENDS: tr fr pr sh cl gl th br st ch

1. _______ ousers

2. _______ iffs

3. _______ etty

4. _______ ings

5. _______ all

6. _______ om

7. _______ eakfast

8. mu _______

9. _______ addest

10. tou _______

C. Circle all the *s* or *sh* letters.

She sells seashells at the sunny seashore.

D. Circle all the *p* letters:

Peter Piper picked a peck of pickled peppers.

E. In the poem "Lament," five words begin with *p*. What are they?

1. _______________________

2. _______________________

3. _______________________

4. _______________________

5. _______________________

LAMENT/AFTERNOON ON A HILL

A. In the poem "Afternoon on a Hill," find and complete the words that begin this way:

1. cl _________________________ **3.** w_________________________

2. cl _________________________ **4.** w _________________________

B. Some people have names that are alliterations.

For example: Susan Simon, Maria Montoya, Hans Hendricks

Can you think of more names that are alliterations?

1. ____

2. ____

3. ____

4. ____

5. ____

C. Write phrases or sentences about ways to spend an afternoon. Use alliteration with the given sound.

1. *k* sound

____

____

2. *r* sound

____

____

3. *p* sound

____

____

D. On a separate sheet of paper, illustrate one of your phrases. What kind of mood does the sound that is repeated help create? Can you express that mood in your drawing?

HOME

A. Which of these belong in the house? Which belong outside?

chimney	porch	gate	basement
driveway	closet	den	balcony
fence	attic	fireplace	kitchen

INSIDE   **OUTSIDE**

______________________   ______________________

______________________   ______________________

______________________   ______________________

______________________   ______________________

______________________   ______________________

B. In which room do these items usually belong?

refrigerator	shower	stove	oven
pillow	mattress	coffee table	detergent
medicine cabinet	tub	shampoo	couch

BATHROOM   **KITCHEN**

______________________   ______________________

______________________   ______________________

BEDROOM   **LIVING ROOM**

______________________   ______________________

______________________   ______________________

C. Which is your favorite room in your home? Use your five senses to help you describe your favorite room and express the reasons for your choice.

____

____

____

HOME

A. In "home," Gwendolyn Brooks uses words other than *said* when the characters speak. Look at the following synonyms for *said*. Then choose the correct definition from the box below.

> said loudly
> let out one's breath audibly
> gave sudden expression of emotion
> said further
> admitted, acknowledged, conceded

1. burst out ____

2. added ____

3. sighed ____

4. allowed ____

5. exclaimed ____

B. Using the synonyms for *said* from above, complete these sentences.

1. Mother _____________ , "Oh, I don't know what to think."

2. "Watch out!" she _____________ .

3. "Buy some milk and cheese. Don't forget some bread, too," she _____________ .

4. "Well, that is the funniest thing I ever saw," she _____________ laughing.

5. "Hmmm, you may be right after all," he _____________ .

C. Write a sentence of your own using these synonyms for *said*.

1. burst out ____

2. added ____

DREAM VARIATIONS/THEME FOR ENGLISH B/
from MONTAGE OF A DREAM DEFERRED

A. Similes are comparisons using *like* or *as*. Complete these similes from the poems in your textbook using the list of phrases below.

a heavy load	a syrupy sweet
rotten meat	a raisin in the sun
darker rivers	

1. Does it dry up like _________?

2. Does it stink like _________?

3. Or crust and sugar over like _________?

4. Maybe it just sags like _________?

5. Like _________
The streets are dark.

B. Metaphors also compare, but they do not use *like* or *as*. Metaphors usually use verbs of being, such as *am* or *is*. Complete the following metaphors with the words listed below.

mouse	key	stars
fruit	sun	wave

1. "I am the _____________," said the king.

2. The quiet girl whispered, "I am the _____________ in this class."

3. One hundred dollars was the _____________ of his hard work.

4. The young lover sighed, "Oh, my love, you are the _____________ shining the way in the dark night."

5. The teacher said, "A book is a _____________ that opens doors to knowledge."

6. The announcer shouted, "A _____________ of people is running onto the football field.

C. Now, complete these sentences as similes or metaphors.

1. She danced into the room like a _____________________________.

2. The boy was a _____________________ in his math class.

3. My house is a _____________________ to me.

FOG

A. In the space below, draw a picture of fog. Think about the kind of mood fog creates. Then write a few sentences to describe your drawing.

____

____

____

____

____

____

____

B. Think of another mood, such as lonely or frantic. Is there an incident or an object that expresses that mood well? Write a short poem that conveys that mood.

____

____

____

____

____

The Pasture/The Road Not Taken/ Stopping by Woods on a Snowy Evening

A. In "The Road Not Taken," Robert Frost describes two roads. Match the descriptions below to the two roads. Some descriptions may fit both roads.

a. grass grows on the road.

b. has not been walked on this morning

c. not many people have walked on it

d. looks like a good road

e. bends

f. this road was taken

THE FIRST ROAD	**THE SECOND ROAD**	**BOTH ROADS**
______	______	______
______	______	______
______	______	______

B. Circle the right choice so that the paragraph tells what the poet was saying in the poem.

There was a road that diverged into (one, two, three) roads. The poet (could, could not) see where the roads went. At first, the poet wanted to travel (the first, both) road(s). So he stood there for a (long, short) time. He looked down the first road. Then he looked down the other road and thought it looked just as (good, bad). He even thought the (first, second) road might be better because it was grassy and (didn't, did) look as if it had been used much. Both roads had been (made, used) before. (Nobody, Somebody) had taken either road that (morning, evening). The poet decided to choose the (grassy, worn) road. He (wanted, didn't want) to come back to try the other road someday in the future. But he knew that he (would, would not) probably ever come back to try it. He took the road that was (less, more) traveled. Making that decision (changed, didn't change) his life.

LILY DAW AND THE THREE LADIES

A. Fill in the missing prepositions in this paragraph from "Lily Daw and the Three Ladies," by Eudora Welty. Choose your prepositions from the list below.

into	from	in	in
between	under	without	with

Lily sat _____________ them _____________ her hair combed and

pinned up _____________ a figure-eight knot _____________ a small

blue hat _____________ flowers. She wore a thin made-over black dress

_____________ Mrs. Watts's last summer's mourning. Pink straps

glowed through. She had a purse and a Bible and a cake _____________

a tin box, all _____________ her lap.

B. Match these characters from the short story with their descriptions.

has milky-yellow hair and a scar on her throat
is the Baptist preacher's wife
works at the post office
works at the store
wears widow's black

1. Mrs. Watts ____

2. Mrs. Carson ____

3. Aimee Slocum ____

4. Lily Daw ____

5. Ed Newton ____

C. Who is your favorite character in the story? Why? Write a short paragraph about this character. Be sure to describe his or her personality. You may also want to use some events from the story as examples.

____

____

____

____

____

THE STILL ALARM

A. Here are stage directions from the play _The Still Alarm_, by George S. Kaufman. Fill in the prepositions from the box.

1. crosses _____________ table

2. knock _____________ hall door

3. A low whistle _____________ surprise

4. pulls out handful _____________ change

5. suitcase _____________ hand

on
to
of
in
of

B. Draw a picture of what you think the set would look like from _The Still Alarm_. Write a few sentences to describe the set.

INVASION FROM MARS

A. Describe each setting by completing the sentences with the phrases listed below.

is where Professor Person hides
has stripes
is where the space ship lands
is where the orchestra is playing

are placed under martial law
is the location of the radio studio
has a huge telescope

1. Hotel Park Plaza ____.

2. The observatory at Princeton _______________________________________.

3. Mars ____.

4. Grovers Mill, New Jersey, ____.

5. Counties of New Jersey ____.

6. New York City ____.

7. An empty house near Grovers Mill __________________________________.

B. Use the words listed below to complete the description.

tentacles   quiver and pulsate   wriggling

gleam   wet leather   saliva

bear   lips

Something's _____________ out of the shadow like a gray snake. Now it's another one, and another. They look like _____________ to me. There, I can see the thing's body. It's large as a _____________ and it glistens like _____________. The eyes are black and _____________ like a serpent. The mouth is V-shaped with _____________ dripping from its rimless _____________ that seem to _____________.

C. Draw a picture of the above description.

Name _________________________________ Date _________________

INVASION FROM MARS

You, too, can make a story come alive to the listeners of a radio drama. Here is a passage from "Invasion from Mars." Write your own vivid adjectives in the blank spaces. Do not use the same word twice.

This is the scene Professor Person sees when he enters New York City after the Martians have attacked it.

I reached Fourteenth Street, and there again were _______________ powder and _______________ bodies, and _______________ smells from the gratings of the cellars of some of the houses. I wandered up through the Thirties and Forties; I stood alone on Times Square. I caught sight of a _______________ dog running down Seventh Avenue with a piece of meat in his _______________ jaws, and a pack of _______________ mongrels at his heels. He made a _______________ circle around me, as though he feared I might prove to be a _______________ competitor. I walked past shop windows, displaying their _______________ wares to _______________ sidewalks—past the Capitol Theater, _______________, _______________. I watched a flock of _______________ birds circling in the _______________ sky. I hurried on. Suddenly I caught sight of the hood of a _______________ Martian machine gleaming in the _______________ sun. I climbed a _______________ hill above the pond at Sixtieth Street. From there I could see, standing in a _______________ row along the mall, nineteen of those _______________ Titans, their cowls empty, their _______________ arms hanging limp by their sides.

FUTILITY

In "Futility," Mary S. Hawling, says that she wishes she could describe rhythm, like the wind "bending down a tree," or color, like "the sky surging bronze and flame," or emotion, like a wild bird that "takes wing and writes a poem across the sky."

Here is your chance to be a poet and create word pictures of rhythm, color, and emotion. Be sure to use vivid nouns, adjectives, and verbs.

Rhythm shows movement.

1. What have you seen that makes a fast, pounding movement?
   (Example: arms thrust out from the crowd at a rock concert)

   ____

2. What have you seen that makes slow, sweeping movements?

   ____

Color can invoke feelings.

3. Use several words for a color that makes you think of something hot. (Example: blinding white heat)

   ____

   ____

4. Use several words for a color that makes you think of something cool.

   ____

   ____

Comparing to nature can explain motion.

5. What things found in nature make you think of anger?
   (Example: a swollen volcano ready to explode)

   ____

   ____

6. What things found in nature make you think of laziness?

   ____

   ____

Name ____ Date ________________

THE SECRET

You are familiar with the organization of paragraphs in a story. The use of stanzas in poetry is something like that. There are nine stanzas in "The Secret." A **stanza**, or verse, is two or more lines of poetry grouped together. They offer only one thought, action, image, or emotion.

Stanzas, like paragraphs, may be arranged chronologically (in the order things happen), by subject matter, or in a logical series. Stanzas often, though not always, have rhyming words at the end of each line. (Poetry that does not rhyme is called **free verse**.) Sometimes, stanzas have **alliteration,** the repetition of certain beginning sounds.

Stanzas may differ in tone and mood, sometimes within the same poem. Often the rhythm of words is part of the poem's overall effect. When a poem is successful, readers are not aware of the many ingredients that go into making a poem and its stanzas.

A. Fill in answers to the following questions about the above reading.

1. The use of stanzas in a poem is sometimes like the use of ______________ in a story.

2. A stanza is ______________ or more lines of poetry grouped together to offer one

______________ , ______________ , ______________ or ______________ .

3. Like paragraphs, stanzas may be arranged in the order things ______________ , by

______________ matter, or in a ______________ series.

4. Stanzas may have ______________ words at the end of their lines. They may differ

in ______________ or mood, sometimes within the same poem.

5. ______________ is part of a stanza's overall effect.

6. Many ______________ go into making a successful poem.

B. Discuss the following questions related to "The Secret" with your partner or group. Afterward, write the responses that seem best to you, as well as your own responses.

1. What do you think the girls' secret might have been? ______________

____

2. What kinds of secrets might teenagers in all societies and cultures share? ______________

____

THE SECRET

Words that mean very nearly the same thing are known as **synonyms**. For instance, many words express almost the same idea as the word *said*. These include *stated*, *reported*, *declared*, and *explained*. In fact, one expert has come up with about one hundred different ways to express *said*.

All these words are synonyms for *said*. However, some have different shades of meaning. Sometimes, the word *whispered* could be a synonym if the speaker spoke softly. *Shouted* might be a synonym if the speaker was loud. *Repeated* might be right if the speaker had said the same thing before—or was quoting someone else.

Using a thesaurus, find synonyms for these words. Some of them are from "The Secret." Underline those that are nearly exact synonyms. Circle those that have similar, but slightly different, shades of meaning.

1. **beautiful:** attractive , pretty, handsome winsome , fair , fine nice good-looking , graceful

2. **wrote:** ____

____

3. **told:** ____

____

4. **talk:** ____

____

5. **oration:** ____

____

6. **sermon:** ____

____

7. **address:** ____

____

8. **speech:** ____

____

9. **behavior:** ____

____

10. **increase:** ____

____

SNOW/UMBILICAL/CUMULUS CLOUDS

Figures of speech help to paint word pictures for the reader. When done well, they make the reader see what the writer sees.

Two colorful figures of speech commonly used are personification and onomatopoeia.

Personification is giving human characteristics to nonhuman beings or things. In "Snow," the poet uses personification when she writes that fenceposts wear hats.

Onomatopoeia is the use of words that sound like their meaning, for instance, *buzz, whiz, bang, pop, pow, plop, bang, jingle*. Many sounds of animals—*meow, moo, woof*—also fall in this category.

You have already learned about other figures of speech—metaphor and simile. A metaphor is a figure of speech that states that one thing is something else. (My love is a red, red rose.)

Similes say one thing is *like* (or *as*) something else. (My love is like a red, red rose.)

Hyperboles greatly exaggerate real situations. They are true but overblown. ("I've told you a million times not to exaggerate!")

A. In the following sentences from "Snow," "Umbilical," and "Cumulus Clouds," determine what figures of speech are being used. Write your answer in the space provided.

1. The bushes in their nightgowns are kneeling to pray. _______________

2. The trees have silver skirts and want to dance away. _______________

3. The title of the poem "Umbilical" refers to the use of transistor radios. _______________

4. I can't live without that sound that sound that sound that *sound*. _______________

5. I can do without sunshine, I can do without spring, but I can't do without my ear to that thing. _______________

B. In the last few years, many new communication devices have appeared. With a partner, list as many new devices as you can think of. On a separate sheet of paper, place this list in one column labeled "Communications Devices." Then label a column next to it, "Effects on Society." This column should tell how the device has changed American habits. One that should come to mind is e-mail, which makes it possible to send messages all over the world in an instant.

TWO KINDS *from* THE JOY LUCK CLUB

Adding a suffix to a word changes the meaning of the root word. For example, the word *play* when used as a noun means "something fun." Adding the suffix *-ful* to *play* turns it into an adjective meaning "full of fun, or not serious."

A. Choose a suffix from the list below to add to the root word in parentheses and write the new word in the blank to complete the sentence.

-able	-ing	-ful	-ed	-ment	-ly	-ent	-less	-ion	-ize

1. (remark) The young child's piano playing was _________________ .

2. (differ) Playing the piano before an audience was _________________ than playing alone.

3. (real) Mother did not _________________ how scared I was.

4. (power) Anger is a _________________ emotion.

5. (list) Hot, humid weather can make you feel _________________ and tired.

6. (reflect) The _________________ in the mirror was of a young girl.

B. Sometimes, you have to change the spelling of a root word when you add a suffix. In the following words, change the *y* to *i*, or drop the *i*, and add the suffix in parentheses to make a new word. Then write the meanings of the new words.

1. saucy (ness) ____

____

2. memory (ize) ____

____

3. lazy (ness) ____

THE WORLD IS NOT A PLEASANT PLACE TO BE

Tone is the author's attitude toward the piece he or she is writing; it involves the mood that an author wants to create.

There can be many different attitudes toward the same subject. For example, a story or poem about a blizzard may be formal and stiff, very serious, light and informal, joking and playful, sarcastic and questioning. Some writing is satirical, making fun of the subject. Some writers are very enthusiastic about their material.

A. With your group, discuss the selections in this unit so far and write what you think the tone of each is.

1.   "The Secret" _______________

2.   "Snow" _______________

3.   "Umbilical" _______________

4.   "Cumulus Clouds" _______________

5.   "Two Kinds" _______________

6.   "The World Is Not a Pleasant Place to Be" _______________

B. "The World Is Not a Pleasant Place to Be" suggests that the world would not be a pleasant place to be without someone to hold. With your group, discuss what other things make the world pleasant. What could you least do without? List some of those things here.

____

____

____

____

____

____

____

____

THE WORLD IS NOT A PLEASANT PLACE TO BE

Homophones are words that sound alike but have different spellings and meanings. Usually this is because they began in different languages, with different roots. Over time, pronunciations may have changed. Today, they sound alike but mean different things. For instance, the word *bore* means a person or activity that is not interesting. It is pronounced the same as *boar*, which refers to a member of the pig family. Both words come from different roots in Old English.

A. Using your dictionary, look up the definitions and origins of these homophones. (Put the origins in parentheses.) Many of these words are from "The World Is Not a Pleasant Place to Be."

1. accept ______________________________   except ______________________________

2. there ______________________________   their ______________________________

    they're ______________________________

3. wood ______________________________   would ______________________________

4. be ______________________________   bee ______________________________

5. knot ______________________________   not ______________________________

6. two ______________________________   too ______________________________

    to ______________________________

7. buy ______________________________   by ______________________________

8. tear ______________________________   tier ______________________________

9. beer ______________________________   bier ______________________________

B. Use the following homophones in sentences that show their meanings.

1. accept ____

    except ____

2. wood ____

    would ____

3. be ____

    bee ____

JOURNEY

In a story, **point of view** describes who is telling the story. Several different points of view are possible.

- **First person**—told by a person participating in the story; uses *I, me, my, we,* and so forth.

- **Third-person observer**—told by a person watching the story happen from a certain point; uses *he, she, they,* and so forth.

- **Third-person omniscient**—told by an observer who sees all and knows what the characters are thinking and doing; uses *he, she, they,* and so forth.

- **Second-person observer**—told by an observer, directed to *you.* The pronoun *you* is used throughout, putting the reader directly in the story. Second-person observer is rarely used.

A. Complete the following sentences by filling in the blanks.

1. Point of view refers to the person who is _______________ the story.

2. A person watching the story, using the pronouns *they, he,* and *she,* is talking from the _______________ -person point of view.

3. A person taking part in the action, using the pronouns *I* and *we,* is speaking from the _______________ -person point of view.

4. An observer who sees all and knows all that is going on is the _______________ -person _______________ .

5. When the story is told from the *you* point of view, this is the _______________ -person point of view.

6. The second-person point of view is _______________ used.

B. *Antonyms* **are words that have opposite meanings.** *Bad,* **for example, is the opposite of** *good.* ***Hot* is the opposite of** *cold.*

Using a thesaurus, find two antonyms of the following words from "Journey."

1. excessive: _______________________   3. elevation: _______________________

2. perfect: _______________________   4. obscure: _______________________

JOURNEY

"Journey" is a metaphor for a person's choices in the journey through life.

1. The wide highway at the beginning of the story is a metaphor for the path that most people take. There are many other cars and drivers. It seems to be an easy, but perhaps boring way, at least for the writer.

2. The smaller road is a metaphor for less commonly taken paths in which a person often has to map his or her own way, instead of relying on others. There is some other traffic along this road.

3. The unpaved road or lane is a metaphor for a path infrequently taken by others. Both difficulties and unexpected pleasures increase.

4. The walking path is a metaphor for an even less traveled path. Difficulties and unexpected pleasures increase yet again.

5. The person in "Journey" finds more difficulties as she travels away from the main road. They are those encountered by a person who tries to be different. However, she also finds more pleasure and seems satisfied.

You often have the opportunity to make choices in life. Name one choice that led to difficulties. Explain. Name one choice that led to unexpected pleasures. Explain. The choice could be the same one for both results.

1. difficulties ____

____

____

____

2. pleasures ____

____

____

____

from BLACK BOY

People write **autobiographies**—stories about themselves—to share their experiences with others.

People read autobiographies because they are curious about others. Readers are especially curious about famous people, or those who have had especially interesting experiences. There are sometimes lessons that can be learned from reading about other people, such as what they did to succeed. Everyone has to find his or her own way. However, everyone can get ideas and hints from others about things that work.

If someone is having a hard time, it often helps to discover that he or she is not alone.

In the selection from *Black Boy*, Richard Wright tells about overcoming a very difficult childhood. He was poor and African American. He had to fight his way to the grocery store. He had to learn that the world often is not always a pleasant place to be—as an earlier selection was titled. He had to fight to keep his money, and he learned to do so. He had to continue struggling all his life to achieve his dream of becoming a writer.

Answer these questions about the reading above.

1. Autobiographies are written because people like to share ______________.

2. People read autobiographies because they are curious about ______________.

3. Reading about other people may teach us what they did to ______________.

4. When someone has a hard time, it often helps to find that he or she is not ______________.

5. *Black Boy* describes Richard Wright's difficult ______________.

6. He learned that the world often is not ______________.

7. He struggled to achieve his dream of becoming a ______________.

from BLACK BOY

Paraphrasing means telling a story in your own words. Sometimes this is done to make a brief summary. At other times it is done to put something in simpler words.

A. Below are sentences that paraphrase *Black Boy*. Number them to indicate the order in which they logically explain the story.

________ **1.** His mother says Richard must fight.

________ **2.** Gangs threaten Richard and take his money.

________ **3.** They have no food; their father is gone.

________ **4.** Richard has to shop for groceries for the family.

________ **5.** Richard learns to fight.

________ **6.** Richard Wright is poor and hungry.

________ **7.** His mother tries to joke about their poverty.

________ **8.** His mother says the family must care for themselves.

One of the purposes of writing is **introspection**. This means that a person looks into himself or herself. A person examines his or her behavior and actions and why he or she did certain things. Sometimes keeping a diary helps us see how we are constantly changing and modifying our views.

Writing things down often helps us clarify our own thinking. When we are angry or upset, we say things we may not mean. Writing things down helps us sharpen our own logic and sense of reality.

Writing things down also helps us become aware of some of our own prejudices—about living and other people.

In summary, the more we write, the better we learn to communicate. This is true not only with others but also with ourselves.

B. On another sheet of paper, write a letter to yourself on a topic that you feel very strongly about. Reread it carefully and show it to a partner. See if it communicates what you want it to say. If not, revise it until it is as good as you can make it.

LITTLE THINGS ARE BIG

Nonfiction tells about real people and events. Fiction describes made-up characters and situations. There are several different types of nonfiction.

a. Narrative—a story told by someone who witnessed certain events, or who did research to find out about them.

b. Autobiography—a story about someone's life, written by that person. Autobiography often is in narrative form.

c. Journal—a daily account of things happening to a certain person or organization.

d. Memoirs—a persons's remember-ances about his or her own life. Memoirs are similar to autobiography, except they focus more on public people in public events.

e. Diary—a daily written record of a person's experiences, often very personal.

f. Letters—correspondence between two or more people. Letters often relate personal events, daily happenings, or an exchange of opinions.

A. Match the items below with the definitions above.

_________   **1.** A very personal daily account of a person's feelings.

_________   **2.** A public person's account of his or her life.

_________   **3.** An account of someone's public life as remembered by that person.

_________   **4.** Two people write to each other, exchanging views on various subjects.

_________   **5.** A person writes daily about his reactions to different situations.

_________   **6.** A story told by someone.

When they first come to this country, many people have difficulty communicating in English. They are afraid of making mistakes in speaking and behaving. In "Little Things Are Big," Jesús Colón talks about failing to help someone. He feels guilty about it later, because he had been afraid to make a mistake.

B. Have you ever been afraid to do something because you were not sure how other people would react? What was it? On a separate sheet of paper describe your fears.

WHERE HAVE YOU GONE

Free verse has no rhyme and no regular rhythms. It may use the so-called natural rhythm of speech. It is organized into stanzas or verses, but it uses recurring rhythms and images for its effect.

A. Read the poem "Where Have You Gone." Answer these questions.

1. What phrases and ideas are repeated throughout the poem? (Many of them are synonyms or the same kind of thought.)

____

____

2. Why do you think the title is in the form of a question?

____

____

B. In your group, discuss these questions. Write what you think is a good answer.

1. In "Where Have You Gone," the person who left apparently is a man. What might the ideas expressed in the poem mean? What would happen to the person who remained?

____

____

2. How might the poem have been different if the person who left had been a woman?

____

____

Name _________________________________ Date _______________

EVERYDAY USE

In English, some words may be used as nouns and verbs. For instance, in "We will walk," *walk* is a verb. In "Let's take a walk," *walk* is a noun. You can say, "We will talk" (verb) or "We will have a talk" (noun).

A. In the following sentences, decide whether the italicized words are used as verbs or nouns. Write *N* for noun and *V* for verb.

_______ **1.** He told *lies* about me.

_______ **2.** She *lies* about her age.

_______ **3.** Did you *park* the car?

_______ **4.** Let's play ball in the *park*.

_______ **5.** He will *polish* the floor.

_______ **6.** Her nail *polish* is red.

_______ **7.** Where will they *house* all the visitors?

_______ **8.** They will live in the *house*.

_______ **9.** We saw a *play* at the theater.

_______ **10.** The children *play* on the swings.

Most stories have themes. The **theme** is the major idea of the literary work.

In nonfiction, the author states the position he or she is taking. The topic of discussion is the theme. The facts he or she states support the topic sentence at the beginning.

In fiction, drama, or poetry, the reader often has to infer the theme. The reader draws a conclusion about the author's message by paying attention to how the characters behave and what they say. Sometimes it is obvious that one of the characters is speaking for the author. The reader also sees how the author describes the characters. He or she feels the tone or mood of the story too.

B. Complete the sentences with information from the above selection.

1. The major idea of a literary work is called the _______________.

2. In nonfiction, it is usually easier to find the theme because the author _______________ it directly.

3. The _______________ _______________ in nonfiction often states the theme directly.

4. The reader often must _______________ the theme in poetry or drama.

EVERYDAY USE

As you recall, setting is the time and place in which a story occurs. Many times, the setting affects the tone and outcome of the story.

A. Use a separate sheet of paper to write your answers. Consider the effects of a change of setting on this story. What might the outcome have been if:

1. The family had lived in Hawaii? Why?

2. The family had lived in a wealthy area? Why?

3. The family had been Asian? Why?

Two important parts of speech are adverbs and adjectives.

Adverbs that describe (modify) verbs, adjectives, and other adverbs. They generally answer the question "How?" For example, in, "The boy ran *quickly*," *quickly* is the adverb that tells *how* the boy ran. We could also say that he ran *graceful-* *ly* or *effortlessly*. Adverbs can often be identified by their *–ly* endings, although adjectives sometimes end that way.

Adjectives describe (modify) nouns or pronouns. They often answer the question "What kind?" The *tall* girl, the *tennis* player, the *blue* car all use adjectives.

B. List three words that could be used to complete each of the following sentences. The first one is done for you as an example.

Adverb   **1.** The bird sang ____sweetly, loudly, effortlessly____ .

Adjective   **2.** The ____________________________ rose bloomed.

Adverb   **3.** The girl talked ____________________________ .

Adjective   **4.** The ____________________________ athlete did well.

Adverb   **5.** He looked at me ____________________________ .

Adjective   **6.** The ____________________________ dogs ran home.

from THE WOMAN WARRIOR

A. Match each description on the right with a statement on the left. Descriptions may be used more than once.

________ **1.** These characters grow during the story.

________ **2.** These characters are more understandable, because readers know more about them.

________ **3.** These characters do not change during the story.

________ **4.** These characters often have conflicting emotions and moods.

________ **5.** These are more likely to be minor characters.

________ **6.** These characters sometimes behave contradictorally.

a. Round characters are fully developed. Readers understand them as whole people. They are more likely to be major characters in the story. Often they have conflicting emotions and moods. They sometimes behave in contradictory ways.

b. Flat characters are not fully developed. Readers know them only as minor characters. Their motivations are not clear.

c. Static characters do not change throughout the story. They are generally the same in the end as in the beginning.

d. Dynamic characters change during the story. Some characters learn new lessons. They grow as they change.

B. Read the excerpt from *The Woman Warrior*. List the characters next to the appropriate type.

1. Round characters ____

2. Flat characters ____

3. Static characters ____

4. Dynamic characters ____

THIS IS JUST TO SAY/THE TERM

Antonyms are words with opposite or nearly opposite meanings. Few antonyms are exact opposites in meaning. Many words carry unique and subtle connotations. Therefore, look for words whose meanings are as close to opposite as possible.

A. Match each word with its antonym.

1. _____ recall		**a.** hopeful
2. _____ sorrow		**b.** defeat
3. _____ futile		**c.** loss
4. _____ recurring		**d.** modern
5. _____ collect		**e.** forget
6. _____ victory		**f.** joy
7. _____ win		**g.** restrict
8. _____ traditional		**h.** final
9. _____ liberate		**i.** improvised
10. _____ planned		**j.** scatter

Free or **open verse** poems are not bound to a structure. They do not rhyme or have a regular pattern. Often, free verse expresses the poet's emotions or thoughts.

B. Write two free verse poems. Make each poem express a different emotion or feeling about something that means a lot to you. Give each poem a title.

_______________________   _______________________

_______________________   _______________________

_______________________   _______________________

_______________________   _______________________

_______________________   _______________________

_______________________   _______________________

_______________________   _______________________

_______________________   _______________________

_______________________   _______________________

_______________________   _______________________